Whole Illu... ... Sous Vide Cookbook:

Complete sous vide recipes with appetizing photos to see what comes out!

Table of Contents

About Whole Illustrated!

This Cookbook is the 2nd book of famous Whole Illustrated cookbook series of genius author Sam Anderson. As in the previous book, here you will find attractive Illustrations and delicious photos of Sous Vide dishes. Though the complete information about Sous Vide cooking which is determined in the previous cookbook, it is a duty of the author to provide some main tips and benefits in the 2nd book also. The Whole Illustrated series are famous with its unique editions, so the same is about this one with full colored paperback version!

Introduction

In the world of professional and home cooking, there are new emerging techniques that simply revolutionize the way we prepare food and come with their own benefits. One of such techniques is what the French call "Sous Vide".

So what exactly Sous Vide refers to and why it has to be used? Sous Vide is French cooking method that calls for cooking food sealed in plastic bags slowly in high temperatures to make the food more tender, flavorsome and evenly cooked.

Many argue that Sous Vide fundamentals aren't as new as we think.

In fact, there are numerous reports that date back to the Ancient Times, where people in various cultures e.g. Egyptians, Romans would tightly wrap food in dense cloths and slowly cook it under steady temperatures/heat until the food had reached the desired cooking point.

The modern Sous Vide era as we know has started in the 1970s where French food experts and chefs were looking for a cooking method to minimize product loss when preparing foie gras and other culinary ingredients. They have specifically found that by sealing the foie gras in plastic bags and slowly cooking it on steady heat, the final result was a more vibrant, tasty, juicy and wholesome. Since that period, chefs from all over the globe have followed and experimented with this technique and today there are several sous vide machine makers that make sous vide cooking a piece of cake for both professionals and home cooks.

It's no wonder why Sous Vide has become a chef favorite, especially in fine-dining and gourmet restaurants, as it really has many advantages over other cooking methods such as:

- **Totally cooking.** Unlike traditional methods like grilling and frying, the heat doesn't reach directly only some parts of the ingredient e.g. a T-bone steak and doesn't need any turning of sides and angles to achieve a uniform cooking result. As the product is sealed and deprived of air, the heat is indirectly distributed evenly.

- **Entire control of doneness.** Modern sous vide machines (even home level ones) allow the slow cooking Sous Vide process to be done using set temperatures and time the cook can freely choose e.g. 300F/140C for 6 hours. Once set, the cooking machine will do the rest and you do not need to check the food doneness every 30 minutes or an hour, like in case of traditional ovens or grilling machines and barbeques.

- **It's easy to prepare meals in advance.** If you don't have the time or energy to spend cooking flavorsome and juicy meals for you or the whole family, you can easily prepare your next day's meal in advance with minimal preparation time and let it cook slowly on its own for some hours.

- **It gets you professional results every single time.** One of the secrets of established chefs used in their restaurants is certainly sous vide cooking. Up until a few decades ago, home sous vide cooking machines were not available in the market but now there are several models on offer that suit any type of cook or budget. If you want the same proportionate, flavorsome and juicy results you can only get in a fine restaurant, it will be better to invest in Sous Vide cooking machine.

So how can you get started with Sous Vide cooking?

The easiest and most direct Sous Vide method that yields professional results every time is the use of a Sous Vide cooking machine with plastic sealable bags and vacuum sealing. However, these machine kits are often costly and the average price for a home unit is $150. However, if you wish to save some cash and buy the essential tools separately here is what you should get:

- **An immersion circulator**. This is a separate tool that you place into a pot filled with water on heat to speed up the heating process and achieve a certain temperature, which the tool displays back.

- **Cambro containers.** These work alongside an immersion circulator and are special plastic containers, which allow better heat insulation compared to a pot when heated. The biggest cambro containers can be filled up to 10 liters and are quite cheap to buy.

- **A vacuum sealer.** This is necessary for sealing and air-proofing the bags that contain the food out of any air that would otherwise ruin it and lead to a speedy boiling process. You can do so on your own by submerging an airless Ziploc bag with the food in a container filled with water but if you want to make sure that no air is present inside the bag with the food, you have to get a vacuum sealing machine.

- **A Cast Iron Skillet.**

In the case of meats or fish, the last optional step to make sure that you have a deep brown crust and a natural looking result and flavor is to finish it off in a heated cast iron skillet, which is an eco-friendly material and great conductor of heat.

If you are using a Sous Vide Kit or machine, it would be wise to check manufacturer's instructions first as machine features vary from one brand to another. However, the basic technique will remain the same: air tightening the bags with the food, setting and displaying the temperatures with a special tool, and using a pot or container that you will submerge the sealed bag with the food inside.

What types of food can you cook with Sous Vide?

In general, Sous Vide cooking works in almost any type of food – from eggs and veggies to meats and seafood. The most common and popular uses of Sous Vide cooking though are for these ingredients:

- Multiple steak cuts e.g. T-bone, Sirloin, New York Strip, etc.

- Pork Chops
- Pork belly
- Beef roast cuts
- Lamb legs
- Chicken thighs and breasts
- Big "meaty" fishes like tuna or salmon
- Shrimps, Lobster and mixed seafood
- Foie Gras
- Hard veggies e.g. potatoes, carrots or brussel sprouts

It is possible to cook some ingredients Sous Vide but not as the main ingredient in a recipe as these types of food are too tender and may fall apart when slowly cooked. Such ingredients that can be used only to enhance the flavor of the meal and in low amounts include:

- Dark leafy greens e.g. spinach, arugula.
- Fruits that contain a high amount of water e.g. oranges, melons, and berries.

- Skin-on cuts like chicken wings or whole chicken (the skin may turn mushy and rubbery when cooked).

Basic Sous Vide Cooking Time & Temperatures

Even though in this Book, you will find some detailed steps and temperatures for each recipe, it would also be useful to know these basic cooking times and temperatures for popular cooking ingredients, based on the doneness you wish to get:

Ingredient	Cooking Time	Temperature ranges
Beef steak (medium rare)	1-1 ½ hour	136F/58-60C
Beef Roast (well done)	5-8 hours	158F/70C
Tough beef cuts e.g brisket or beef chuck (medium)	20-24 hours	158F/70C
Pork Chops (well done)	1 ½-3 hours	158F/70C
Pork Roast (well done)	3-4 hours	158F/70C
Chicken flesh e.g. thighs or chicken breasts (tender and juicy)	1-3 hours	149F/65C
Bone in chicken cuts	3 hours	149F/65C
Big fish fillets e.g tuna, salmon (tender and flakey)	40 minutes to an hour	122F/50C
Green Vegetables	10-15 minutes	185F/85C
Root vegetables e.g potatoes, carrots.	2-3 hours	185F/85C

Shrimps and shellfish	10-12 minutes	140F/60C

Generally speaking, the tougher an ingredient is e.g. beef brisket, longer it will need to cook, while more naturally tender and delicate it is, the less time and temperature it will need.

Using extras like fat/oils or herbs will not alter the cooking results or temperatures but may prove useful for enhancing the whole flavor of the recipe and perhaps making it more emollient.

Recipes

Breakfast

Creamy Egg Bites

TOTAL COOK TIME: 30 min

INGREDIENTS FOR 6 SERVINGS

- 6 large eggs
- 1 cup of heavy cream
- ⅓ cup cottage cheese
- Pinch of salt

- Optional topping e.g. chopped tomatoes, herbs, bacon bits, sour cream.

METHOD

- Heat up the immersion circulator/joule to 185F/85C and place on a pot filled with enough water to cover 6 medium sized mason jars.
- In a big bowl crack the eggs and add the heavy, cream, cottage cheese, and salt. Blend everything together till you end up with a light orange/yellow and uniform liquid.
- Distribute the egg mixture into the 6 mason jars filling them up to 90% of their capacity (around one inch left towards the upper lid).
- Close tightly the mason jars
- Cook for 25-30 minutes
- Let cool for at least 10 minutes before serving and add your toppings of choice to add some texture and flavor.

NUTRITIONAL INFORMATION (Per Serving)

Calories: 210

Carbohydrate: 1.96 g

Protein: 10.66 g

Fat: 17.54 g

Fluffy Ham & Eggs Scramble

TOTAL COOK TIME: 15-18 min

INGREDIENTS FOR 2 SERVINGS

- 4-5 eggs
- 4 stalks of asparagus, trimmed and cut diagonally
- ¼ red bell pepper, sliced
- ¼ sweet onion, chopped
- 1 tbsp of butter
- 2 oz. of cooked ham
- 2 tbsp of heavy cream
- Salt/pepper

METHOD

- Fill up with water and preheat the sous vide container at 168F/75C.
- In a medium skillet, add the butter and saute for 5-7 minutes the asparagus first. Add the peppers and onions and saute for another 2-3 minutes or until softened (but not browned).
- Place all the ingredients e.g. ham, eggs, herbs and veggies into a Ziploc bag and seal using an air tightening machine.
- Soak in the water container and let cook for 15-18 minutes. Massage the content with your hands (wear heat proof gloves first) every few minutes to make sure you end up with a uniform egg scramble and then return to the water bath.
- Remove the eggs from the bags and serve in 1-2 hot plates.

NUTRITIONAL INFORMATION (Per Serving)

Calories: 418

Carbohydrate: 9.38 g

Protein: 24.53 g

Fat: 31.36 g

French Toast

TOTAL COOK TIME: 1 HOUR

INGREDIENTS FOR 4 SERVINGS

- 4 slices of white bread
- 2 whole eggs
- ½ cup heavy cream
- ¼ cup butter
- 1 tsp of vanilla extract
- ½ tsp of cinnamon powder

METHOD

- Beat together the eggs, the heavy cream, the vanilla and the cinnamon in a bowl.

- Soak the bread slices in the egg/milk mixture.
- Insert the bread slices and the remaining mixture in a sous vide pouch.
- Set the cooking time for 1 hour/147F.
- Finish off the bread slices in a greased pan to give them a golden brown toasted appearance.
- Serve with maple syrup or honey (optionally).

NUTRITIONAL INFORMATION (Per Serving)

Calories: 289

Carbohydrate: 13.62 g

Protein: 7.91 g

Fat: 22.49 g

Orange/Lemon yogurt

TOTAL COOK TIME: 3 HOURS

INGREDIENTS FOR 4 SERVINGS

- ½ cup of plain yogurt
- 1 liter of full-fat milk
- ½ tsp of orange zest
- ½ tsp of lemon or lime zest

METHOD

- On a stovetop, heat the milk to around 180 F.
- Remove from heat and let cool to a room temperature
- Add in the yogurt and mix with a spatula.
- Add the citrus zest and stir well.

- Transfer the mixture into 4 glass mason jars.
- Set the Sous Vide temperature at 115F, add the mason jars to the pod or container of the machine and cook for 3 hours.
- Let cool and chill before serving

NUTRITIONAL INFORMATION (Per Serving)

Calories: 168

Carbohydrate: 13.33 g

Protein: 8.75 g

Fat: 8.98 g

Easy Poached Eggs

TOTAL COOK TIME: 12 min

INGREDIENTS FOR 2 SERVINGS
- 4 large eggs
- Salt/Pepper

METHOD
- Using your temperature circulator, set the temperature to 167F/75C in a water-filled Dutch oven or plastic container.

- Using a heaped spoon, gently lower each egg in the water bath (no pouch needed), cover and cook for 12 minutes.
- Fill a large bowl with ice water and transfer the cooked eggs to the ice bath gently to firm them up.
- To serve, transfer the eggs into small individual bowls and season with salt and pepper to taste.

NUTRITIONAL INFORMATION (Per Serving)

Calories: 92

Carbohydrate: 0.75 g

Protein: 6.32 g

Fat: 6.85 g

Lunch

Juicy Sirloin Steak and Yukon Potatoes

TOTAL COOK TIME: 1 ½ HOUR

INGREDIENTS FOR 4 SERVINGS

- 4 sirloin steaks
- 2 pounds of baby Yukon potatoes (or similar potato variety)
- 1 tbsp of steak seasoning

- 4 tbsp of butter
- Salt/Pepper

METHOD

- Place the potatoes in a pot with boiling water and cook for 10 minutes
- Add the butter and season with salt and pepper to taste. Keep in a bowl and set aside.
- Set the sous vide machine to 130F/54C.
- Season the steaks with salt and pepper and the steak seasoning and add to air tightened Ziploc bags.
- Submerge in the preheated sous vide container and let cook for 1 hour and 15 minutes (for a medium rare cook). Remove from the Ziploc bags and strain excess juices with a strainer
- Grease a pan with a bit of oil or butter and sear the steaks for 1 minute on high heat on each side.
- Serve in a dish with cutted Yukon potatoes.

NUTRITIONAL INFORMATION (Per Serving)

Calories: 330

Carbohydrate: 40.88 g

Protein: 11.2 g

Fat: 14.05 g

Pulled Pork Tacos

TOTAL COOK TIME: 16 HOURS

INGREDIENTS FOR 5 SERVINGS

- 2 ½ pounds pork shoulder
- 10 corn tortillas
- 1 onion diced
- 1 bunch of cilantro
- 3 tbsp of taco or fajita seasoning
- Salt/pepper to taste

METHOD

- Set the immersion circulator temperature to 165F/74C.
- Season the pork shoulder with the taco seasoning. Make optionally small incisions with a knife so that the seasoning can penetrate inside.
- Place the pork shoulder on a vacuum bag and air tight.
- Add to the heated water bath and cook for 16 hours.
- Remove from the heat, drain excess liquids and place in the broiler of your oven for 20-25 minutes to form a thin brown crust.
- Shred the pork shoulder with a fork and a knife. Serve over the corn tortillas and some chopped cilantro, onion and optionally tomato slices on top.

NUTRITIONAL INFORMATION (Per Serving)

Calories: 372

Carbohydrate: 54.6 g

Protein: 65.61 g

Fat: 47.68 g

Chicken Marsala

TOTAL COOK TIME: 1 ½ HOUR

INGREDIENTS FOR 4 SERVINGS

- 4 chicken breasts
- 1½ sprigs of fresh thyme
- ¾ cup Marsala wine
- ¾ cup chicken stock
- 3 cups sliced white mushrooms
- 3 tbsp butter
- 1 tbsp of fresh parsley
- Salt/Pepper to taste

METHOD

- Combine all the ingredients except the mushrooms, butter and parsley in a Ziploc or sous vide bag and air tight.
- Set the sous vide heater to 141F/64C
- Submerge the bag with the chicken and liquids in the water bath.
- Cook for 1 hour and 15 minutes.
- While the chicken breasts cook, saute the mushrooms in melted butter and season with salt and pepper to taste.
- Once the chicken is cooked, remove from the bag and drain excess liquid.
- Transfer on a serving dish and add the mushroom sliced and parsley on top for garnish.

NUTRITIONAL INFORMATION (Per Serving)

Calories: 428

Carbohydrate: 0.63 g

Protein: 91.87 g

Fat: 19.24 g

Lemon & Dill Salmon

TOTAL COOK TIME: 45-50 min

INGREDIENTS FOR 2 SERVINGS

- 2 skinless salmon fillets
- 1 tbsp of roughly chopped dill
- 1 lemon, cut into slices
- ½ tsp chilli flakes
- 1 tbsp of olive oil
- Salt/pepper

METHOD

- Set the immersion circulator tool at 135F/58C in a water-filled container.
- Place the salmon fillets in a Ziploc bag and seal with a sealing machine.
- Submerge into the heated water bath and cook for about 50 minutes (for a medium cooking result).
- Remove from the bag and serve ideally with cooked brown rice or asparagus.

NUTRITIONAL INFORMATION (Per Serving)

Calories: 176

Carbohydrate: 1.74 g

Protein: 34 g

Fat: 10.64 g

Shrimps with Wine, Tomato and Garlic

TOTAL COOK TIME: 40 min

INGREDIENTS FOR 5 SERVINGS

- 1 ½ pounds peeled shrimp
- 6 tbsp of extra virgin oil
- ⅓ cup tomato paste
- 1 tbsp of smoked paprika
- 6 cloves of garlic, minced
- 1 bay leaf
- 2 tbsp of sweet wine

- Salt/Pepper

METHOD

- Set the sous vide cooking temperature at 140F/60 (for a 90% opaque and tender shrimp cooking result).
- In a skillet, add all the olive oil and garlic, follow with the wine, and add the rest of ingredients except the shrimp.
- Add the shrimps in a large plastic bag and add the tomato wine mixture, lightly tossing to distribute evenly.
- Cook for 45 minutes before serving. Serve ideally on a shallow baking dish with rice and some veggies.

NUTRITIONAL INFORMATION (Per Serving)

Calories: 411

Carbohydrate: 9 g

Protein: 40.25 g

Fat: 23.49 g

Dinner

Mint & Garlic Lamb Chops

TOTAL COOK TIME: 2 ½ HOURS

INGREDIENTS FOR 5-6 SERVINGS

- 2 racks of lamb, excess fat and fibers removed
- 3 cloves of garlic
- 2 tbsp of chopped fresh mint leaves
- 1 tbsp of olive oil
- Salt
- Freshly ground pepper

METHOD

- Set the sous vide temperature to 135F/60-62C.
- In a small bowl, combine the olive oil, the mint leaves, the garlic and salt/pepper and mix well.
- Brush the mixture generously onto the lamb racks.
- Cook for 2 ½ hours (for a medium result).
- Remove from the bags and serve ideally with arugula salad and/or baked baby potatoes.

NUTRITIONAL INFORMATION (Per Serving)

Calories: 250

Carbohydrate: 0.46 g

Protein: 29.01 g

Fat: 14.77 g

Butternut Squash & Apple Soup

TOTAL COOK TIME: 2 HOURS

INGREDIENTS FOR 4 SERVINGS

- 1 medium butternut squash, peeled and sliced
- 1 large green apple, seeds removed and sliced
- 5 green onion, chopped
- ¾ cup heavy cream
- Salt/Pepper

METHOD

- Set the immersion circulator to 185F/85C in a container filled with water.
- Combine all the ingredients except for the cream and apples in a large Ziploc bag and seal.
- Cook for 2 hours.
- Remove from the bag and blend in a large soup bowl with an immersion blender.
- Add a few drizzles of heavy cream or olive oil on top as well as the apple slices and serve.

NUTRITIONAL INFORMATION (Per Serving)

Calories: 122

Carbohydrate: 14.85 g

Protein: 1.79 g

Fat: 7.15 g

Mayo & Beetroot Garnished Scallops

TOTAL COOK TIME: 32 min

INGREDIENTS FOR 2 SERVINGS

- 6 fresh scallops, cleaned and drained well
- 1 tbsp of extra virgin olive oil
- 1 large beetroot, peeled and roasted
- ¼ cup mayo
- 2 cloves of garlic
- 1 tbsp of lemon juice
- 1 tbsp of fresh dill, chopped

- ½ cup baby arugula leaves

METHOD

- Set the sous vide cooking tool temperature at 122F/56C inside a water container filled 80% (of its capacity).
- Add the scallops, salt, pepper, and olive oil in the Ziploc bag and seal with a sealing machine.
- Let cook for 30 minutes.
- While the scallops cook, roast in the oven at 300F/150C the beetroots with the garlic. Remove from the oven, mash with a fork and set aside.
- Once the scallops cook, remove from the bag and heat a skillet with a bit of butter. Sear the scallops for 1 minute on each side to get a light golden brown crust.
- Serve with the garlic, beetroot puree, mayo, and the arugula leaves and finish off with a drizzle of lemon juice and dill on top.

NUTRITIONAL INFORMATION (Per Serving)

Calories: 241

Carbohydrate: 8.89 g

Protein: 11.8 g

Fat: 17.81 g

Mediterranean Style Octopus

TOTAL COOK TIME: 6 HOURS

INGREDIENTS FOR 4-5 SERVINGS

- 1 medium fresh octopus
- 1 tbsp of olive oil
- 1 tsp of thyme
- 1 tbsp of dried oregano
- ¼ cup white dry wine
- 2 cloves of garlic
- ⅓ cup fresh parsley, chopped
- Salt/Pepper

METHOD

- Clean the octopus well with water and a brush and remove the head.
- Cut off the octopus suckers and place on a deep bowl.
- Add the olive oil and the herbs with the garlic (except the parsley) as well as the wine and marinate for at least an hour before cooking.
- Set the sous vide machine circulator at 160F/78C on the container filled with water (there should be a few inches left till full).
- Cook for 5-6 hours. Strain from excess liquids.
- In a greased grilling pan, add the octopus to sear for 2 minutes on each side on high heat.
- Serve with some chopped parsley on top and optionally an extra drizzle of olive oil.

NUTRITIONAL INFORMATION (Per Serving)

Calories: 376

Carbohydrate: 9.66 g

Protein: 61.35 g

Fat: 8.45 g

Sage Turkey Breast & Carrots

TOTAL COOK TIME: 4-5 HOURS

INGREDIENTS FOR 3-4 SERVINGS

- 1 whole turkey breast skinned
- 2 tbsp of fresh sage leaves
- 2 cloves of garlic
- 1 tbsp of olive oil
- ¼ cup vegetable stock
- 1 tbsp of corn flour
- Salt/Pepper

METHOD

- Mix together all the ingredients except the corn flour in a deep bowl. Let marinate in the fridge for at least 2 hours.
- Set the temperature of the immersion circulator (or sous vide machine) to 135F/56C and let heat over a water-filled container.
- Take a Ziploc bag and add the turkey breast with the marinade. Seal using a vacuum sealing machine.
- Submerge the bag with the turkey in the heated water and let cook for 4-5 hours.
- Drain from the liquids and reserve them in a small bowl and transfer the turkey alone onto a serving dish. Slice into 1 inch thick pieces
- Take all remaining liquids and add the corn flour to make a light gravy. Season with salt and pepper to taste.
- Pour the gravy on top of the turkey breasts.

NUTRITIONAL INFORMATION (Per Serving)

Calories: 988

Carbohydrate: 0.8 g

Protein: 136.17 g

Fat: 44.79 g

Dessert

Poached Pears with Red Wine Sauce

TOTAL COOK TIME: 1 HOUR and 25 min

INGREDIENTS FOR 3-4 SERVINGS

- 4 ripe pears
- 1 bottle of high quality dry red wine (around 3 cups)
- 3 tbsp honey
- 1-2 sticks of cinnamon
- 1 tbsp of super fine white sugar

- 1 cup of heavy cream

METHOD

- Set the sous machine circulator and filling machine (with 90% of water) to 176F/80C.
- In a saucepan, combine all the ingredients together except the pears. Stir well and let simmer for 15-20 minutes. Reserve.
- Peel, remove the seeds and cut the pears in halves. Place in a sous vide bag with half of the wine mixture and seal preferably with an air-tightening sealing machine. Let cook for an hour.
- Separate the liquid from the pears in the bag and transfer with the rest of the wine sauce in a saucepan.
- Heat until you get a syrup-like consistency and pour over the pears in a deep serving dish.
- Serve optionally with whipping cream on top.

NUTRITIONAL INFORMATION (Per Serving)

Calories: 119

Carbohydrate: 30.4 g

Protein: 1.55 g

Fat: 0.29 g

Espresso Ice Cream

TOTAL COOK TIME: 3 HOURS and 20 min

INGREDIENTS FOR 4-5 SERVINGS

- 1 tbsp of instant espresso powder dissolved in ½ cup of hot water
- 1 cup of white sugar
- 5 egg yolks
- 1 ½ cup heavy cream
- 1 tsp of salt

METHOD

- Fill the container with water and set the sous vide cooking machine to 140F/60C.
- Blend with an immersion blender or hand mixer the sugar and egg yolks together until smooth. Slowly mix in the heavy cream and the salt as the blender operates.
- Transfer the mixture onto a large bag and use a sealing machine ideally to remove air and seal it completely.
- Submerge in the heated water and let cook for 20 minutes.
- In a separate bowl, get some chilled water with ice and submerge the bag with the cream mixture (do not open) to cool down the temperature.
- Open the bag and transfer the mixture to a plastic ice cream container or ice cream maker and let in the freezer for at least 3 hours prior serving. If you don't have an ice cream maker, beat with a hand mixer the cream as it firms up every 20-30 minutes to achieve a fluffy ice-cream texture.
- Serve in small ice cream glasses or pots.

NUTRITIONAL INFORMATION (Per Serving)

Calories: 324

Carbohydrate: 27.46 g

Protein: 4.33 g

Fat: 22.34 g

White Chocolate Creme Base

TOTAL COOK TIME: 1 ½ HOUR

INGREDIENTS FOR 4 SERVINGS

- 1 cup of heavy cream
- 1 cup of semi-skimmed milk
- 5 oz. of white chocolate, roughly chopped
- 1 gelatine leaf, dissolved in cold water
- 1 tsp of salt

METHOD

- Preheat the sous vide water bath to 180F/90 C.

- Chop the white chocolate into rough small pieces, place in a vacuum bag and seal with an air tightening machine.

- Once the white chocolate is done, heat 1 cup of the milk to around 110F/50C. Drain out any excess fluid from the gelatine and add to the milk, using a whisk to dissolve it.

- Transfer the white chocolate mixture to a bowl and whisk well until you achieve a paste. Use a hand mixer to gradually mix in the heated milk.

- Once all the milk has been mixed, chill in the fridge for 30 minutes. Beat again using a hand mixer and return to the fridge for at least an hour before serving. If the mixture isn't fluffy enough, mix for another time with your hand mixer.

- Serve ideally with some caramelized apple or pear or pineapple slices and some nuts or nut crumble and even granola.

NUTRITIONAL INFORMATION (Per Serving)

Calories: 325

Carbohydrate: 24.77 g

Protein: 4.71 g

Fat: 23.68 g

Flourless Chocolate Cake

TOTAL COOK TIME: 1 HOUR

INGREDIENTS FOR 4 SERVINGS

- 4 large eggs
- ½ cup semi-sweet chocolate chips or squares
- 4 oz. of butter
- 1 tbsp of coffee liqueur e.g. Kalua
- 2 tbsp of cocoa powder (for dusting the cakes)

METHOD

- Have your water bath ready and set the sous vide temperature tool at 115F/46C.

- Combine the chocolate butter and coffee or liquor in a sealing bag, seal with an air tightening machine and submerge in the heated water for 20 minutes, until the chocolate has melted.
- Remove the bag and adjust the temperature to 170F/76C.
- Lightly grease with butter 4 mason jars.
- In a mixer bowl, beat the eggs on high speed until fluffy and around double in volume.
- Switch the speed to low and gradually introduce the melted chocolate mixture until everything looks uniform.
- Take a large spatula and scrape the final mixture onto the mason jars making sure it is distributed evenly.
- Close the lids of the jars tightly using your hands.
- Place them carefully into the preheat water bath for an hour or so.
- Remove them carefully one by one using gloves or towel and place over a rack. Let chill for at least 20 minutes.
- Using a sharp flat knife, remove the cakes from the jars cutting all over the sides.
- Transfer onto small dessert dishes and garnish optionally with some berries or chocolate whipping cream.

NUTRITIONAL INFORMATION (Per Serving)

Calories: 300

Carbohydrate: 9.27 g

Protein: 8.57 g

Fat: 26.09 g

Apricot Jam

TOTAL COOK TIME: 2 HOURS

INGREDIENTS FOR 4 SERVINGS

- 12 oz. of dried apricots
- 1 ½ cups of granulated sugar
- 1 cup of water
- 1 lemon, juiced (zest kept)

METHOD

- Set the sous vide temperature heating tool to 190F/87C.

- Combine all the ingredients in a vacuum seal bag and seal ideally with a machine.
- Submerge in the water bath and cook for 2 hours.
- Transfer the apricot mixture in clean mason jars.
- Let chill for at least 20 minutes and refrigerate or store in a cool and dry place for up to 3 months.

NUTRITIONAL INFORMATION (Per Serving)

Calories: 179

Carbohydrate: 46.22 g

Protein: 0.45 g

Fat: 0.11 g

Drinks

Cold Brew Coffee

TOTAL COOK TIME: 2 HOURS

INGREDIENTS FOR 2-3 SERVINGS

- ½ cup fresh coarse coffee
- 4 cups of water
- Coffee strainer or filter

METHOD

- Set the sous vide temperature tool to 150F/65C and make sure that the water level covers around ¾ of the container.
- Combine ½ cup of the coffee with 4 cups of water and distribute the coffee mixture onto two large mason jars.
- Tighten the lids using your hands.
- Place the jars onto the heated water bath for 2 hours.
- Open the jars and pass through the brewed coffee through the filter. Let chill in the fridge for at least two hours prior serving.

NUTRITIONAL INFORMATION (Per Serving)

Calories: 1

Carbohydrate: 0.07 g

Protein: 0.02 g

Fat: 0.01 g

Sous Vide Eggnog

TOTAL COOK TIME: 1 HOUR

INGREDIENTS FOR 4 SERVINGS

- 8 whole eggs
- 4 egg yolks
- 4 cups of milk
- 3 cups of heavy cream
- 1 cup of white sugar
- 1 tsp of vanilla bean of extract
- 2 cinnamon sticks
- 1 tsp of nutmeg powder (freshly ground)
- 2 cups of bourbon whiskey

METHOD

- Set the sous vide tool to 144F/ 62C in a container filled 80% with water.
- Combine the egg yolks, the eggs, the heavy cream, the milk, sugar and vanilla extract in a blender.
- Place one cinnamon stick into the bottom of a mason jar (4 mason jars in total).
- Pour the cream mixture onto the jars. Add the whiskey (half cup for each jar) and stir. Tighten the jars up with your fingers.
- Place the jars onto the water bath for 1 hour.
- Serve with some ground nutmeg on top.

NUTRITIONAL INFORMATION (Per Serving)

Calories: 856

Carbohydrate: 68.58 g

Protein: 23.44 g

Fat: 54.49 g

Spiced Rum

TOTAL COOK TIME: 2 HOURS

INGREDIENTS FOR 6 SERVINGS

- 1 bottle of rum
- 2 whole cloves
- 1 tsp vanilla extract
- 2 whole black peppercorns
- ½ piece star anise
- 1 tsp of orange zest

METHOD

- Preheat the sous vide machine filled with water at 153F/67C.
- Transfer the mixture into a vacuum seal bag, seal and submerge in the water bath for 1 hour.
- Transfer back to the bottle or serve in 5-6 six small cocktail glasses.

NUTRITIONAL INFORMATION (Per Serving)

Calories: 412

Carbohydrate: 0.12 g

Protein: 0.01 g

Fat: 0 g

Sous Vide Limon cello

TOTAL COOK TIME: 2 HOURS

INGREDIENTS FOR 10 SERVINGS

- 10 fresh, unwaxed lemons
- 4 cups of vodka
- 4 cups of water
- 1 ½ cups of superfine sugar

METHOD

- Set the immersion circulator at 135F/57C.

- Take a peeler or grater and remove the zest in the form of strips from the lemons, making sure that no white flesh is peeled as well. Reserve the lemons for later use.
- Insert the peeled lemon zest strips inside a vacuum seal bag with the vodka. Seal using a vacuum machine.
- Submerge in the water bath and cook for 2 hours.
- Meanwhile, combine the water with the sugar in a saucepan until you make a thin syrup. Mix with the vodka lemon grind mixture.
- Serve chilled.

NUTRITIONAL INFORMATION (Per Serving)

Calories: 91

Carbohydrate: 6 g

Protein: 10.16 g

Fat: 5.27 g

Raspberry Mint Iced Tea

TOTAL COOK TIME: 30 min

INGREDIENTS FOR 8 SERVINGS

- 2 liters of water
- 8 tsp of loose green tea leaves
- 1 cup of crushed raspberries
- 30 fresh mint leaves

METHOD

- Set the sous vide temperature heating tool at 140F/60C.

- Combine all the ingredients inside a vacuum seal plastic bag (except the leaves) and seal ideally using a vacuum sealing machine.
- Submerge the bag into the heated water and cook/brew for 30 minutes.
- Once done, pass through the liquid through a strainer, chill for at least 20 minutes and refrigerate for 2-3 hours before serving with ice cubes.

NUTRITIONAL INFORMATION (Per Serving)

Calories: 29

Carbohydrate: 7.48 g

Protein: 0.29 g

Fat: 0.04 g

Conclusion

Once you have invested in a sous vide cooking kit or machine, you'll realize that there are countless of recipes to try out to get chef-worthy results at home, easily and with minimal preparation.

There are no strict rules when it comes to cooking sous-vide, however, if you wish to make the most of your sous vide cooking experience, here are some additional tips that will help:

- Sear your meats before or after cooking sous-vide. If you don't want to get that soft-boiled taste or texture, it's best to sear your meats e.g. pork chops or even chicken thighs on a greased grill pan before placing into the Ziploc or vacuum sealing bag.

- Make sure that the Ziploc bag or vacuum pouch is fully sealed using a machine ideally, as any trapped air will alter the results and lead to a soft-boiled effect in texture whilst diluting the flavor of the ingredients.

- Placing the bag in the freezer for 10 minutes is ideal to draw out any excess moisture before placing the ingredients of the recipe inside. This will also make the vacuum sealing process much easier.

- Even though the cooking time may vary from one ingredient to another (check the table on chapter 1 for more details) the exact temperature will remain the same regardless and so it is highly unlikely that your meats especially will overcook (well unless you cook for 36 hours in a row).

- Since sous vide often involved using liquids inside the pouch/bag to achieve a more juicy and tender texture, instead of tossing these liquids away, reserve and make a sauce or gravy using 1 tbsp. of cornstarch for every cup of liquid kept. You can add optionally some butter, herbs and salt/pepper for taste to finish up your sauce and pour over the cooked food.

- Due to the presence of liquids in most of the sous vide recipes, it is not indicated that you keep the food outside at room temperature for more than 2 hours as bacteria may spread out quicker than other types of dry food. If you won't be serving the dishes immediately, refrigerate (up to 3 days) or even freeze.

- Cooking your food for more than 48 hours is excessive and most chefs agree that it doesn't lead to better results e.g. in the case of tough meat cuts like briskets or leg lambs.

- Don't over-vacuum the pouches in recipes where you want to achieve fleshy and flaky results e.g. salmon or cod dishes. If the fish or ingredient is delicate and needs less cooking time than others, leave a small space for the juices to freely flow inside.

- Once you have learned the basic of cooking sous-vide, expert chefs suggest to use two separate heat settings depending on the type of food you are cooking. You will set the first temperature halfway through the cooking process and switch to the second for the remaining half cooking process. Here are some basic temperature indications:

38-43°C (100-109°F): Very rare to rare tuna

49-55°C(120-130°F): Medium-rare to medium fish and shellfish

39-49°C(101-120°F): Rare to medium-rare salmon

55-60°C(131-140°F): Beef medium

60°C-65°C (140°F): Pork and chicken cuts

82-85°C (180-185°F): Root vegetables e.g. carrots, cauliflower, beetroots.

63-65°C (145-149°F): Poached eggs

- Don't over-season the key ingredient e.g. meat or fish fillet with too many herbs, spices or extras as they won't only lose their color and vibrancy, they may overpower the natural flavor of the dish and this isn't what you are looking for. In general, dry spices work better than fresh ones texture-wise but you can add tiny amounts of small herbs if you wish to enhance the aromas and flavor without exceeding 1-2 tbsp. per 500 grams of a key ingredient.

In general, sous vide cooking leaves plenty of room for experimentation and there is no such thing as overcooking your dish, especially when it comes to preparing savory dishes with meats as your base. The given temperatures are indicative and are based on the results you wish to achieve e.g the doneness of the meat or fish. Therefore, it makes sense to alter the cooking temperatures to get a different cooking result as opposed to altering the time, as in many cases cooking it more won't necessarily change things. The only time when cooking time matters is when preparing egg-based dishes and creamy desserts or jams, as these will take some time to yield silky smooth results.

We hope you have found all the tips and recipes useful. We believe that with a little bit of practice, you are on your way of preparing restaurant quality dishes that are rich in flavor and texture, and will surely impress your family and guests.

Made in the USA
Lexington, KY
20 October 2018